STANDARD BEARER
International Ministries

John 17:17

Divine Strategies for Prophetic Watchmen
By D.J. Carmouche

Published by
Standard Bearer International Ministries
Printed in USA
All rights reserved

I0099323

For booking or orders
Contact Dana Carmouche
Standard Bearer International Ministries
PO Box 300382 • Houston, TX 77230
Email: dana@sbiministries.org
www.sbiministries.org - www.shop.sbiministries.org

ISBN: 978-0-6158191-3-6
Copyright 2013 © SBIM
All rights reserved

Reproduction of text in whole or in part, via ALL electronical or mechanical devices, without the expressed written consent of the author is not permitted and is unlawful according to the 1976 United States Copyright Act, except for the inclusion of brief quotations in a review.

Unless otherwise indicated, all scriptural quotations are from the New American Standard Version of the Bible.

Scriptures marked (AMP) are from the Amplified New Testament, ©1954, 1958, 1987, by the Lockman Foundation; or are from the Amplified Bible, Old Testament, ©1962, 1964 by Zondervan Publishing House.

Scriptures marked (ESV) are from The ESV® Bible (The Holy Bible, English Standard Version®) copyright © 2001 by Crossway, a publishing ministry of Good News Publishers.

Divine Strategies for Prophetic Watchmen

TABLE OF CONTENTS

These strategies are designed to be used interactively as you seek Adonai for revelation and understanding, coupled with the Word of G-d. These strategies are intended for use as a spiritual building tool and are not intended to supplant your relationship with Adonai nor your responsibility to "study to show yourself approved."

DEDICATION

This book is dedicated to ALL of the mid-wives who have labored alongside me on my journey to bring forth G-d's Divine will for my life. These women have taught me how to PUSH beyond the pain to bring forth LIFE. It was skills acquired in my wilderness that prepared me to be an effective warrior in the army of the Lord.

Thanks to Mrs. Barbara Hicks, Pastor Suzette T. Caldwell, Minister Patricia Eugene, Pastor Sandra Hall, Minister Taunya Malone, Pastor Carolyn Hayes, Dr. Cassandra Scott, Apostle Deborah Anderson and Mother Gloria Gorrell for correcting, counseling, comforting & coaching me through my labor pangs and thrusting me into my destiny.

I want to extend a very special blessing of thanks to the most important mid-wife in my life, my mother, Mrs. Ezia Mae Fuller. In her quiet strength, I learned how to stand amidst opposition and to KEEP IT MOVING!

Thank you to all those who impacted my life either positively or negatively, I learned from BOTH.

Love Dana

Chapter 1

PREPARING AN ARMY FOR WARFARE

When you go out to battle against your enemies, and see horses and chariots and people more numerous than you, do not be afraid of them; for the LORD your G-d is with you, who brought you up from the land of Egypt.

Deuteronomy 20:1

I t was the summer of 2011 and I was entrenched in the heat of battle. It wasn't a physical battle, but rather an intense spiritual battle. In the twinkling of an eye, the Lord called my best friend and rock home. I lost my sister to cancer in June and a few months later, my dad to a heart attack coupled with throat cancer. What I remember vividly about their passing was the numbness and disconnect that I felt. I had prayed and fasted for some time on their behalf; warring against forces in unseen realms, but my desired end was not to be. At that moment, I felt like King David when he prayed for the Lord to spare the life of his first born, but the Lord allowed the child to die.

It was during this time that a deeper intimacy with G-d was birthed and I fully understood how to trust and depend on HIM. I was tested in this season, like Job; the enemy desired for me to curse G-d and die, but what the enemy didn't know was that G-d was preparing me for WARFARE. This warfare was one that required total submission to the Lord and unwavering FAITH in HIS word.

Warfare is defined as "armed conflict between two massed enemies, armies, or the like *(Dictionary.com)*. Therefore, as "good soldiers" we must be prepared for this conflict with our enemy, the adversary.

In Revelation 7:9, we see an equipped army of the Lord prepared to engage the enemy of our soul in warfare. When you enlisted into the Army of the Lord, there were certain benefits that were afforded you by the King. In HIS sovereignty, we were assured that during our "exodus" **none** would be worn or weary *(Jer. 12:5)*, nor ANY feeble among the armies of the Lord *(Psalms 105:37)*. My dad & sister had run their course and are NOW part of the Lord's eternal army!

THE ARMY OF THE LORD

There are requirements necessary to be an effective soldier and advance the Kingdom of G-d. Several biblical examples are provided as a blueprint of how to prepare to engage the enemy of our soul. Let's examine Joshua's journey to better understand what it takes to be used by the Lord and be a prepared sol dier in the "army".

Joshua's journey begins in Exodus 17, where Moses instructed him to go out and fight Amalek, the descendant(s) of Esau. His obedience to the words of Moses proved to be victorious, in that Joshua and the army of Israel overwhelmed the Amalekites with the sword.

Here we see Joshua's ability to submit to authority IN obedience. According to Jeremiah 35, **OBEDIENCE** is a requirement in order for you to be used effectively in the Army of the Lord. Joshua's submission to G-d's appointed authority in the earth realm and his faithful obedience to the instructions given to him, opened doors that NO MAN could close. This victory revealed another facet of G-d the Father... and Israel was able to see Jehovah Nissi, G-d our Banner! ONE simple act of obedience caused Joshua to be promoted in the Army of the Lord and later leader of G-d's people.

Today's leaders must be like Moses and groom the next generation of Joshua's to lead the Army of the Lord. G-d instructed Moses to chronicle this victory over the Amalekites, as a memorial and to rehearse it in the ears of Joshua...for the Lord was going to remove the memory of Amalek from the earth **(Ex. 17:14).** Likewise, allow those under your command to experience intense battles so that at the appointed time, they will be effectively prepared soldiers equipped to be used by G-d.

True warriors are in position and they fully obey G-d's word...AT ALL COST! You must also be zealous for the things of G-d. I love the story of Phinehas in **Numbers 25:11,** because of his zeal toward the things of G-d, Phinehas was able to stay the hand of the Lord. Have you been able to turn the hand of G-d from what HE intended to do, simply because HE saw your zeal?

EQUIPPED FOR THE BATTLE

As warriors, we are **EQUIPPED** for spiritual warfare and therefore must operate efficiently in the spiritual realm. This is achieved through a process which ALL warriors must endure. It begins with us being clothed with the Holiness of G-d *(Lev. 20:7)* and fighting according to the Lords instructions; so that we may be strengthen in the battle *(Judges 7)*. In addition to being equipped, we must also be prepared to fight *(1 Cor. 14:8)*. At the sounding of the trumpet by the watchman, we must be swift to the battle, armed with the "full armor" of G-d *(Eph. 6:10)*, while operating in **GREAT** Faith.

As we continue to examine Joshua's journey, we see that his equipping for battle was wrought in his submission to G-d's authority, coupled with his willingness to stand amidst opposition. Because of his obedience, Moses identified Joshua as a future leader of Israel. In Numbers 13-14, Joshua along with Caleb **BELIEVED** the report of the Lord, even when a million people disagreed. As a soldier in the Army of the Lord, you must **TRUST** the word of G-d above any other word or voice.

As a prepared soldier, you are required to have an intimate relationship with the Lord. Joshua's fellowship allowed him to move beyond natural circumstances into G-d supernatural provision.

In Exodus 33, Joshua communes with G-d; not only when his mentor is around, but long after Moses had departed the tabernacle. Therefore, your **PRIVATE** worship does have a **PUBLIC** platform *(Matt. 6:6).* It was the intimacy that Joshua experienced in those quite moments with G-d that prepared him to be used of the Lord; to lead the people of Israel to the promise land. He had witnessed Moses spending time communing with G-d, and "worship" beckoned him to engage G-d for himself.

There were many battles fought and won as the children of Israel journeyed through the wilderness in pursuit of the "promised land", and Joshua learned how to deal with varying personalities, while pressing pass fatigue to pursue what G-d had promised. Even in his elevation, Joshua remained faithful and submitted to G-d's authority in the earth realm.

The **SET TIME** had come for Joshua to execute the strategies, insight and wisdom that he acquired while walking with Moses for 40 years. The on-the-job training that Joshua received, equipped him for the battles yet to come. In Joshua 6, G-d gives Joshua instructions to take Jericho, and because he faithfully submitted to Moses during their Exodus from Egypt, he was equipped with the skills to bring the children of Israel across the Jordan. His battle against Amalek, intimacy and unwavering trust in G-d's word, prepared him to lead the children of Israel into what G-d had already declared was theirs.

FIT FOR THE MASTER'S USE

FEAR from a psychological perspective is a natural biochemical reaction necessary for us to detect danger. The "fight or flight" response that our physical bodies experience causes us to prepare to enter combat.

Equally opposite to the biochemical reaction of fear is our emotional reaction. The fear experienced in our emotions stifles our creativity and opens up the door to doubt and unbelief in the Word of G-d.

Deuteronomy 20: 5-9 provides specific battle instructions prior to warfare engagement.

Then the officers shall speak to the people, saying, is there any man who has built a new house and has not dedicated it? Let him go back to his house, lest he die in the battle and another man dedicate it. And is there any man who has planted a vineyard and has not enjoyed its fruit? Let him go back to his house, lest he die in the battle and another man enjoy its fruit. And is there any man who has betrothed a wife and has not taken her? Let him go back to his house, lest he die in the battle and another man take her.' And the officers shall speak further to the people, and say, 'Is there any man who is fearful and fainthearted? Let him go back to his house, lest he make the heart of his fellows melt like his own.' And when the officers have finished speaking to the people, then commanders shall be appointed at the head of the people. *(ESV)*

The first exemption from war dealt with your "new house". Therefore, your house should be dedicated to G-d and engulfed with reverential fear and worship of HIM. By doing so, you allow the presence of G-d to inhabit your praise and HIS Spirit will dwell there. A **wise builder** will always build on a *solid foundation*, which is TRUTH in the Word of the Lord.

- Are you a wise or foolish builder?
  o I Corinthians 3:10
  o Matthew 7:24-27
  o Matthew 16:18
  o Psalm 118:22

The next exemption from war is for those that have planted a vineyard. **Leviticus 19:23-25** indicates that for the first three years, the fruit of any newly-planted vineyard was considered unfit for use, and the fourth year was appointed to bear the first-fruits which were dedicated wholly to the Lord!

For ALL new converts, the Lord provides a time frame allowing Holy Spirit to cleanse you and create a clean heart within you. In the fourth year of your walk, the fruit that you bear will be **"fit for the Masters"** use and presented as a first-fruit offering, dedicated wholly to the Lord!

- Those that planted a vineyard...
  o I Corinthians 9:7
  o Galatians 5:22-23
  o Luke 21:19
  o I Peter 4:8

G-d keeps covenant, even when we are unfaithful. That doesn't mean we have a "free pass", to continue in folly. And because he honors covenant, he made provisions for those who are in covenant with him, which are not altered by time or circumstances...they are ETERNAL.

- The covenant keeper...
  - Deuteronomy 7:9
  - Deuteronomy 24:5
  - II Chronicles 13:5
  - Exodus 19
  - Romans 11

While on our Christian journey, we must continue to fight the good fight of faith, and lay aside every weight that so easily besets us. Verse 9 of Deuteronomy speaks to the fearful among us. Fear is a very deadly enemy toward progression in the Lord's work, but the answer can be found in *I John 4:18*.

- To war the good fight, we must apply the word of G-d!
  - Thessalonians 5:14
  - Psalm 31:24
  - Psalm 27:14
  - Revelation 21:8

As you mediate on these scripture versus, allow Holy Spirit to strengthen you in your inward parts. Let the ALL consuming fire burn up anything in you that's not like HIM. I admonish you to stay on the Master's wheel, becoming the "good soldier" **(II Tim. 2:3)** & continue to fight the good fight of faith; because the battle is not yours...it belongs to the Lord **(II Chron. 20:15).**

Chapter 2

A Watchmen's Charge

*For thus the Lord said to me: "Go, set a watchman; let him
announce what he sees. 7When he sees riders, horsemen in pairs,
riders on donkeys, riders on camels, let him listen diligently, very
diligently." 8Then he who saw cried out: "Upon a watchtower I
stand, O Lord, continually by day, and at my post I am stationed
whole nights.*

Is. 21:6-8(ESV)

The Lookout

rowing up, I was the youngest of 30+ *first* cousins and was
therefore designated as the **"look out"**. My *charge* in the
natural was to look out for my great aunt *{Noon}* and to let
them know when she was approaching. So in other words, I had to
sound the alarm of her advance. Long before I read the above
scripture or accepted Jesus as my Lord *and* Savior, G-d the Father
knew that I would be a watchman. At an early age I was honing my
watchman skills, which would prove useful when I became born
again. It was during these days that I learned to listen diligently for
footsteps and the sound of someone approaching. Fast-forward to
2013 and you will find me vigilant and attentively listening for
impending danger and awaiting instructions from the Lord.

Watch

...but all the people shall keep the watch of the Lord.
II Chron. 23:6b, (KJ21)

Every believer is instructed to keep [the watch], notice it
didn't say [a watch]. This is stating a specific rather than general
assignment. According to Ezra, the Scribe, "all" are to watch, but
"all" *are not* watchmen.

To watch is *[Mishmereth],* meaning {guard post, charge, function, ward, safeguard, & service division}; but to be a watchman; *[Tsaphah] or [Shamar]* means to {preserve; to guard from danger, to hedge up, to keep watch, & watch closely}.

WATCHMAN

"Son of man, I have appointed you a watchman to the house of Israel; whenever you hear a word from My mouth, warn them from Me.
Ezekiel 3:17(NAS)

Watchmen are prophetic intercessor OR prophets that are commanded to "keep watch" **{Tsaphah}** & "preserve" **{Shamar}.** This verse informs us that the Lord *can* appoint a [watchman] to preserve your life and the lives' of those around you. As an **appointed watchman**, you are to preserve your city, state, church, & nation by warning the believers of impending danger. If they heed not your warning, then they will perish in their own iniquity. But as G-d's appointed watchman {prophet}, if you fail to warn of impending danger, the blood will be REQUIRED of you...

SO PROPHETS SHAMAR!

- Guard/Protect/Preserve
- Have charge of
- Heed/Hedge up
- Attend to/Care for/Tend to
- Observe/Pay attention
- To keep (within bounds)
- Sabbath/Covenant/Command
- Watch for/Treasure up

The **watchman** *{prophet}* is charged with the responsibility of guarding & protecting the house. This house refers to your physical, natural and spiritual house. The watchman's responsibility is to hedge up the city, state & nation at the gates, preserving it from all impending danger.

By **discerning** what spirits have entered your region; you can entreat G-d for the strategy to defeat those demonic forces and preserve the house from harm *(Ezk. 33: 6-8).* The strategy could be praise, prayer, preaching, teaching and/or worship *[studying the word of G-d]*...but ALL must be coupled with intimacy with the Father.

In order to assist you with your study on the word Shamar, let's examine the "Law of First Mention" *LOFM*. This simply refers to the first time a word is mentioned in the Holy Scriptures, which is our ultimate authority. With regard to Shamar, the LOFM is Gen. 2:15, where G-d instructed Adam to guard & keep the garden.

> *And the Lord G-d took the man and put him in the Garden of Eden to tend and guard and keep it.*
> *G e n e s i s   2 : 1 5   (A M P)*

Shamar can also refer to guarding/tending to the sheep (the people of G-d). The same word is used for guarding the mouth and keeping the heart {Psalms141}. It also refers to the hedging of a nation...the KINGDOM! So **prophets/watchmen** are needed to **Shamar** and protect nations.

Just as the armed forces are charged with the task of protecting/guarding the USA from both domestic and foreign attacks; in like manner, as a **watchman**/prophet you are called to **Shamar**/guard the gates of your city/nation from ALL demonic activity. Each of us is called to safeguard, watch and be at our division of service. Those with the grace to Shamar must begin to SHOUT from the roof-tops what the Lord is saying, so that generations can be preserved from impending danger.

Therefore, the **specific** assignment of a watchman is to be vigilant with keen discernment, allowing for a clear visual of the approaching enemy. **G-d instructed us to "watch" in *prayer** [Mk. 13:37, I Pt. 4:7, Lk. 12:34, Jer. 31:28, Col. 4:2, Lk. 21:36, & Mt. 26:40-41].*

DECLARATION FOR DISCERNMENT

Father I pray NOW that You release discernment upon your people, I declare that they have keen discernment and an eagle's eye in the spirit realm Lord'. Allow these your sons to see farther than they've ever seen before. I thank you Adonai; that YOU are bringing everything into alignment in this season of their lives. Release upon them Abba the anointing that's upon my life; that they may see beyond dimensions and time. Anoint their eyes to discern friend and foe as the move forward advancing the Kingdom.

Selah!

A WATCHMEN'S SET PLACE

Also I set watchmen over you, saying, Hearken to the sound of the trumpet...
J e r e m i a h   6 : 1 7 (A S V)

As watchmen, we are to stand guard over our **SET** place. In the above scripture from Jeremiah, we see that the Lord set Jeremiah as a watchman over Israel, to warn them of impending danger. The word **"set"** means to position yourself and be aware that Satan will attempt to cause you to move out of your **set** place. **Daniel 7:25** informs us that Satan will endeavor to change the set times and laws, attempting to discourage and prevent you from taking your place in the watchtower. But you must take an attitude of being unmovable and stand in your assigned place to fulfill your destiny.

A **set place** can include your church, home, business, and/or geographical location {city, state, region & nation}. Your assignment as a watchman is to *sound the trumpet* and **warn** the believers of **ALL** spiritual activity that is operating illegally in the territory. When you sound the TRUMPET, **declare** what you see in the heavenly realm. To be highly effective in this season, stay in your **"set"** place and listen diligently to the voice of the LORD! The Word of G-d commands us to be ALERT and VIGILANT, because the adversary roars around *like* a lion (Judah), seeking whom he may devour *(1 Peter 5:8)*. Thus the adversary attempts to portray himself as the Lion of the Tribe of Judah, but because YOU, as the watchman are *vigilant and alert*, you expose the "father of lies" and warn the believers to turn from the path of destruction and return to the Lion of the Tribe of Judah....Jesus the Christ!

Biblical examples of watchmen in scripture:

Watchmen are **set** in a region (Neh. 7:3)	Watchmen **set** on streets (Ps. 127:1)
Watchmen **set** on towers (II Kings 9:17)	Watchmen **set** in church/temple (II Kings (11:6)
Watchmen **set** on state borders (Is. 62:6)	Watchmen **preserve** order (Song of Solomon 3:3; 5:7)
Watchmen **warned** in times of danger (Jer. 51:12)	Watchmen are **vigilant** (Neh. 4:9; Is. 21:8)
Watchmen **sounded** the alarm (Ezk. 33:2-3)	Watchmen **warned** of those approaching (II Sam. 18:24-27) & (II Kings 9:18-20)

BUILD AMIDST OPPOSITION

*...And conspired all of them together to come and to fight against Jerusalem, and to hinder it. Nevertheless we made our prayer unto our G-d, and **set a watch** against them day and night, because of them.*

N e h .   4 : 8 b - 9

The adversary WILL come to *hinder* your progress...**KEEP IT MOVING ANYWAY**! As a believer, you must expect opposition to the fulfillment of your **DESTINY.** Like Nehemiah, there has to be a resolve within your DNA that compels you to continue amidst the opposition and rebuild the old waste places *(Is. 58:12).* How do you prepare for the opposition? I'm glad you asked...SIMPLE: fortify your gates *(Neh. 7)*. Ultimately, the strategy to overcome the adversary is to *set a watch (Jer. 51:12) &* continue in intimacy, prayer, worship and fasting.

Joshua, like Nehemiah, faced what appeared to be insurmountable challenges when trying to fulfill his G-d given assignment. He was charged with bringing the children of Israel into the Promised Land. Like his predecessor, Joshua was entrusted with the responsibility of ensuring that G-d's people walked in the fullness of what He had destined for them.

For 40 years, Joshua had been able to dialogue with his mentor & leader for advice and sound wisdom. Now here he is, preparing to cross the Jordan River during harvest season with the banks overflowing, but Joshua had a promise from G-d," I will be with you as I was with Moses...Be of good courage"!

There is going to come a time in your Christian journey when you will have to navigate your course without being able to speak with those that have poured into your life. During this time, the perfecting of those skills acquired while walking with your leader; will need to manifest in order to advance the Kingdom of G-d. There is NO quick way through your process! In order to build against every seemingly possible opposition, you must set a watch, and make your prayers unto G-d, so that He can fight your battle.

Like Nehemiah and Joshua, you will also build amidst all of the chaos going on around you. I remember when I became a leader in the private sector and I was the point person on a million dollar project. Outwardly, I may have appeared somewhat young for the task, but what was unknown is that I had been preparing for leadership for a long time. Taking on duties and responsibilities that no one else would, and showing up for functions that weren't my assignment caused me to be recognized. I was demonstrating loyalty and commitment long before the opportunity presented itself. G-d was working in me the patience and tenacity necessary to fulfill the assignment. He knew that a moment would occur, when everything I said and did would be put under a microscope to discredit me and defame my character. But because I had been preparing long before the test, I prevailed victoriously in Jesus Name!

SOUND THE TRUMPET

When you go to war in your land against the adversary who attacks you, then you shall sound an alarm with the trumpets, that you may be remembered before the LORD your G-d, and be saved from your enemies."

N u m .   1 0 : 9   (N A S)

This verse informs us that we **WILL** go to war...so NOW is the time to prepare for the attack. A watchman blew the trumpet to warn of impending danger *(II Kings 9:17); so* the trumpet is symbolic of the voice of the prophet *(Is. 52:8).* The LORD set watchmen over His people and they have the **authority** to sound the trumpet *(Is. 62:6).* The adversary's plans can be stopped when the people respond to the sound of the trumpet. To ignore the trumpet is to **die in your own iniquity (***Ezk 33:2).*

As a set watchman, I'm warning of the impending danger against your soul. REPENT for the Kingdom of G-d is at hand. Know that in this hour, G-d will not be mocked, for surely HE will visit HIS people. The cleansing will begin in the house of the Lord. Therefore, my assignment, is to make ready a people prepared for the KING *(Luke 1:17).*

The sounding of the trumpet was commanded by G-d for the purpose of summoning the people to assemble, signaling the advancement of the camp, declaring war and during times of gladness, solemn days, annual festivals, and the beginning of each month to rejoice over burnt offerings and peace offerings *(first- fruit).* G-d specifically requested that the two trumpets in Numbers 10 be made of beaten silver, meaning every impurity was removed. **Silver** is symbolic of redemption, atonement, righteous and true words in the Bible:

The tongues of those who are upright and in right standing with G-d are as choice silver (Proverbs 10:20a). A word fitly spoken and in due season is like apples of gold in settings of silver" (Proverbs 25:11). The standard currency of the day was shekels of silver which were used for trade. In the same way, words are also traded; they are given and received (often with the expectation of something in return), and some words have more value and worth than others - based upon their weight and clarity.

TWO SILVER TRUMPETS

The LORD spoke further to Moses, saying, "Make yourself two trumpets of silver, of hammered work you shall make them; and you shall use them for summoning the congregation and for having the camps set out.
Num. 10:1-2 (NAS)

The trumpets were two in number, symbolic of their devotion to witnessing. According to scripture, the two silver trumpets could only be blown by the priest and the word declares that we are PRIEST...But you are A CHOSEN RACE, A royal PRIESTHOOD, A HOLY NATION, A PEOPLE FOR G-d's OWN POSSESSION; so that you may proclaim the excellencies of Him who has called you out of darkness into His marvelous light; (I Peter 2:9). In I Corinthians 14:8, the Apostle Paul writes, "If the trumpets give an uncertain voice, who shall prepare himself for war?" So as a watchman, your sound must be clear and precise so that the people will assemble in battle array prepared for war.

SUMMONING THE PEOPLE TO ASSEMBLE

The "silver trumpets" were used to call an assembly together. These instruments established the oneness of fellowship for G-d's people. We also sound the SILVER trumpets in order to stir the hearts of the people and bring them to repentance! When playing a trumpet, the sound is made through three things: the breath, the tongue and the lips - ALL of which are necessary for speaking!

The "trumpets" are a picture of the Word of G-d, so in essence, G-d's voice is likened to a trumpet and the words spoken from G-d's mouth are like pure silver (Psalm 12:6). In **Ex. 19:19** the Lord trumpeted HIS response atop Mount Sinai and in Rev. 1:10, while Apostle John was worshipping in the Spirit, he heard the voice of the Lord like a "trumpet blast". Apostle John goes on to say in verse 4:1, that the same voice was like a "mighty trumpet blast" foretelling of things to come.

All throughout scripture, we see G-d's voice described as a trumpet. Apostle Paul told the Thessalonians, in I Thess. 1:8 "For the Word of the Lord has sounded forth from you, not only in Macedonia and Achaia, but also in every place your faith toward G-d has gone forth". He further encourages the Corinthians (I Cor. 14:6) to prophesy in a language that the church could understand. The **trumpet** had to be clear for people to understand. So too must the gift of prophecy, forth-telling the Word of G-d be clear and understandable for the people to follow.

Avoid anything which would tend to scatter or divide the people of G-d. The ministry of the silver trumpets *(which we all are a part of)* is never to fragment G-d's people but rather to strengthen relationships and unite the body. It is a great ministry to bring the Lord's people together and therefore, the silver trumpets are symbolic of G-d's Word and Message going forth in clarity and purity. So today I release a clarion call for the "prophetic watchmen" to arise and take their rightful position in the body of Christ.

Signaling the Advancement of Camps

The two silver trumpets where coupled with the cloud of Shekinah glory which rested upon the Tabernacle. The pillar of cloud and fire provided guidance for G-d's people, and when Israel was in right relationship with Him, the guidance was always towards the land of promise. When it was time for the children of Israel to move forward, the trumpets were sounded to give direction to march, bringing them into ALIGNMENT WITH G-D's DIVINE PURPOSE FOR THEIR LIVES.

As silver trumpets, we are to govern G-d's people in relation to the ultimate fullness which He has for them in Christ. G-d arranged the 12 tribes in a "distinct" order based on their call, gifting and characteristics. Likewise, each of us should be aligned with people and ministries that allow our callings, gifting and characteristics to be utilized for the edification of the body and glorification of G-d!

At the sounding of the trumpets, the tribes on the East; which were the *fore-runners, course setting* tribes of JUDAH, ISSACHAR and ZEBULUN, would break camp first. When the trumpet was sounded a second time, the tribes on the South; which were the battle-axe brigade tribes of REUBEN, SIMEON and GAD, would break camp next. Smaller blast of the trumpet would signal the tribes on the West, which were the next generation warrior tribes of EPHRAIM, MANASSEH and BENJAMIN and bringing up the rear were the tribes on the North, consisting of DAN, ASHER and NAPHTALI. This is the order that the Lord established by the standard of each tribe.

DECLARING WAR

The sound of the two trumpets prompts us to war…it causes us to contend for our faith and smash down the gates of hell. It reminds us to look at the time and season and ensures that we are moving prophetically, according to the word of G-d (Leviticus 23). G-d is still using silver trumpets today through whom He blows His Breath/Spirit. The sound which comes forth must be distinct and clear, because if the trumpets give an indistinct sound, who will prepare themselves for war? (I Cor. 14:8). Additionally, if someone tries to trumpet forth a message without having been refined, hammered, prepared and created by G-d, they will be like wind that just blows away (Jer. 5:13). Malachi 3:1-3 declares that WE must first be formed into instruments "FIT FOR THE MASTERS USE", through the refining and purifying of the fire of G-d.

DURING OTHER TIMES

The sounding of the silver trumpets is a call to both gladness and mourning. In Psalms 105:8, we see that the sounding of the trumpets is a reminder to G-d of His covenant forever, the word which He commanded to a thousand generations. The blowing of the trumpet reminded G-d to rescue the children of Israel from their enemies (Numbers 10:9). And today's sounding of the trumpet by the prophetic watchmen also puts G-d in remembrance of His Word. Finally, the blowing of the trumpets is a perpetual statute...DECLARING that G-d's Word is eternal!

SIX CHARACTERISTICS OF A WATCHMAN

1. **Intercession** *(Standing in the Gap)*
    a. Spending time in prayer *(Luke 6:12)*
    b. Praying without ceasing *(I Thess. 5:17)*
    c. Praying in the Holy Spirit *(Jude 1:20)*

2. **Discernment** *(The presence or absence of Holy Spirit)*
    a. Detect what has entered into a region *(1 John 4)*
    b. Lifting of Holy Spirit *(I Thess. 5:19)*
    c. Clean & unclean *(Ezk. 44:23)*

3. **Preaching** *(In power & demonstration of the Spirit)*
    a. Walk worthy of the calling (Eph. 4:1-32)
    b. Obedience & submission *(Heb. 13:17)*
    c. In & out of season *(II Tim. 4:2)*

4. **Teaching** *(Thy Kingdom Come)*
    a. Study the word *(II Tim. 2:15)*
    b. Examine the scriptures *(Acts 17:11)*
    c. Spirit & Power of the Most High G-d *(I Cor. 2:4)*

5. **Praise** *(Let everything that has breath, praise the Lord)*
    a. Lift up your voice and shout for JOY! *(Is. 52:8)*
    b. Enter into his courts *(Psalms 100:4)*
    c. With my whole heart *(Psalms 9:1)*

6. **Worship (In Spirit & Truth)**
    a. Rabbinical teaching informs us that *study* is **ONE** of the highest forms of worship.
    b. Worship in Spirit & in Truth *(John 4:24)*
    c. A call to worship *(Psalms 99:5)*
    d. Reason to worship *(James 4:8)*

WATCHMEN ARISE

Father I thank you, for theses your true sons that are being manifested in this hour. Let YOUR Kingdom come and YOUR will alone be done in and through each person praying this prayer. I call forth a stirring in their Spirit that will shift the very foundations; cause the watchman to ARISE. I declare that they no longer slumber as fools, but instead stand alert and vigilant. As set watchman, they will blow the trumpet, so that the people are warned, and preserved from being taken away in their own iniquity. Son of man, the Lord has made you a watchman for the house of Israel [place your home or church]. Whenever you hear a word from G-d's mouth, you shall give warning from G-d!

On the walls, O Jerusalem [Houston, Texas], I have set watchmen; all day and all night they shall never be silent. You who put the Lord in remembrance, take no rest, and "set up a standard against the walls of Babylon. Make the watch strong; set up watchmen; prepare the ambushes; for the Lord has both planned and done what he spoke concerning the inhabitants of Babylon. Now Lord, search us in our inward parts and allow us to know the errors of our folly. Let not presumptuous sin have dominion over us. With humble and contrite Spirits, we come before YOUR throne of Grace. We confess our sins before YOU and turn inward to the path of righteousness today. Continue to make a way of escape from the enemy's devices and schemes. Now unto HIM who alone is able to keep us from falling; do we give ALL Honor, Glory & Dominion.

In Jesus Matchless Name

Chapter 3
BATTLE READY

Lest Satan should get an advantage of us: for we are not ignorant of his devices.
2 Cor. 2:11 (KJV)

Battle ready is a term used in military settings denoting a functional weapon. It is given that term because weapons that are considered **"battle ready"** are made to a *higher standard* than your average display weapon. My question for you today is: "are you battle ready"? Have you allowed the refiners fire to purify and test you; causing you to declare "The LORD is my G-d"? *(Zech. 13:9)* If you have allowed the process of your departure from Egypt to have its perfect work in and through you, then you are battle ready. I envision the Exodus from Egypt as a splendorous event, but equally important was the process of forgetting the former things and pressing toward the mark of the *High Calling (Phil 3:14)*.

The departure from situations and behaviors that held generations before you captive is not an easy feat. It was during the 400 years of slavery that strongholds had taken up resident and squatted on the land that the Lord had declared belong to the children of Israel. Like the children of Israel, our ancestors have allowed strongholds to occupy territory in the crevasses of their mind and passed those generational curses down through the blood line, causing generations to be enslaved. The charge for ALL believers today is to examine your battle readiness, because it is time to go to war against your enemy.

The enemy that you wrestle with in your mind and the demonic forces that have squatted long enough on the territory that G-d has already given to YOU, must be evicted! So how do you evict the enemy? It first begins with you knowing your enemy; you can't be ignorant of the enemy's devices/strategies. You must be aware of how the enemy attacks, when & with what, so that you are fully prepared for the battle. You can no longer allow the enemy to bring a fight to your door; you must bring it to him in this hour!

G-d instructs us as believers to be cognizant of the tactics of our enemy. With those instructions in mind, let's examine the leadership style of Attila the Hun. In A.D. 451, Attila prepared the Huns for battle against his arch enemy Aetius of the Roman Empire. The Battle of Châlons would prove to be Attila's first and only defeat. It is said that after this defeat, Attila reorganized his army to withstand the tactics of his adversary Aetius. These changes implemented; to better prepare his army for battle, came with profound changes in the customs held from generation to generation. Ultimately, Attila the Hun became one of the most revered warriors because of his ability to understand the tactics of his adversary and devise strategies to overcome and prevail during battle.

As soldiers in the Army of the Lord, we too must assess our previous setbacks and revamp our strategies and tactics prior to battle. This will require us praying without ceasing **(I Thess. 5:17),** and being watchful & vigilant because our adversary is roaring like a lion seeking whom he may devour **(I Pet. 5:8).**

RECONNAISSANCE

And the Lord spoke to Moses, saying, Send men to spy out the land of Canaan, which I am giving to the children of Israel; from each tribe of their fathers you shall send a man, everyone a leader among them.
Num. 13:1-2 (NKJ)

Webster defines reconnaissance as "a preliminary survey to gain information; *especially* : an exploratory military survey of enemy territory. First natural then spiritual **(1 Cor. 15:46)**...the fullness of this verse is applicable in our life today. Before any branch of military engages in war, there is a deployment of agents to gather intelligence on the enemy in order to adequately prepare the troops for war. The gathering of this information is referred to as "strategic intelligence".

For the first decade of the 21st century, I was blessed to have a spiritual general training & mentoring me to reign. Under the general's watchful eye and the leading of Holy Spirit, I learned how to employ strategic intelligence and use it to devise a plan to effectively defeat demonic forces. Before I ever began ministering in deliverance, I first had to be delivered from generational curses and self-imposed bondage.

It would be two years before I would even began preparing to walk into my destiny. During my time of preparation, the instructions where simple: **observe, PRAY, fast, PRAY, study the word** and at the end**...PRAY** so more! The word of G-d solidified in prayer, became the foundation on which I stand today. It was during this time of preparation that General Hicks taught me how to examine the character, nature and power structure of my enemy. I learned how to hear the voice of G-d clearly and trust and depend on Holy Spirit for instructions.

Before I began assessing demonic activity in regions & territories, and developing strategic plans for warfare, I FIRST had to submit to authority and allow my mind to be renewed. My character had to be chastened and victorious battle stories were rehearsed in my hearing, to increase my faith **(Ex. 17:14)**. My talents were being sharpened so that when the Lord had need of them, I would be ready. The altar is where I discovered the love and grace of G-d, while in prayer I became aware of G-d's Supremacy and my TOTAL dependency upon Him. I was being groomed for greatness...not for myself, but to lead G-d's people upon HIS command.

Like the spies, I learned how to assess the strategies of the enemy and fulfill the assignment given to me because I was able to submit and pray for those in authority over me **(I Tim. 2:2)**. It was during my intimate times in prayer that I could declare like Joshua, believe the report of the Lord. Joshua was one of 12 spies sent out by Moses to assess the land that the Lord had promised to give to the Israelites. Of the 12, only Caleb and Joshua came back with a report that lined up with the word of G-d. Have you ever felt alone in your stance for the things of G-d? If so, you are in **good** company.

During the time that Joshua walked with Moses, he was able to evaluate how to handle complaints from differing opinions, and apply G-dly wisdom to the situation. In Numbers 14:6, Joshua demonstrates the qualities that had been cultivated during his time of mentorship. I believe that the skills and attributes in Joshua where refined while crossing the Rea Sea; during intimate times with G-d and by observing Moses as he navigated a million people through the wilderness, with various personalities.

KNOW YOUR ENEMY BEFORE COMBAT

...and moreover, we saw the descendants of Anak there. 29"Amalek is living in the land of the Negev and the Hittites and the Jebusites and the Amorites are living in the hill country, and the Canaanites are living by the sea and by the side of the Jordan."
Numbers 13:28b-29

Three years after my exodus, I began ministering to the people of G-d. Like Joshua, I had to wait until the appointed time, while developing the skills necessary to be effective in battle. Joshua's first introduction in scripture is his commanding of the Army of the Lord against the Amalekites. I dare say that in order to be assigned to lead the Army of the Lord, Joshua had to demonstrate some skills that qualified him for the position. His lifestyle and character had to reveal that he was capable to lead, but more importantly that G-d had chosen him to lead.

Let me encourage you today: "be strong & of good courage", because upon your exodus from bondage, the enemy will wage war against you. The first battle that the children of Israel encountered after their Exodus, were the warriors of Amalek. Prior to this battle, I believe that Joshua was being prepared to lead the army of the Lord. Although scripture doesn't indicate, I imagine during the crossing of the Red Sea with Pharos's army in hot pursuit, Joshua's gift made room for him to be noticed by Moses.

In the heat of the battle against the Amalekites, Joshua knew that his leader, the person in authority over him, was praying and seeking the face of G-d for his victory. When Joshua prevailed against the Amalekites, G-d instructs Moses to rehearse this victory in Joshua's hearing as a precedent for future battles.

Chapter 4

THE ART OF WAR: POSSESS THE GATES

*...indeed I will greatly bless you, and I will greatly multiply your seed as the stars of the heavens and as the sand which is on the seashore; and your **seed shall possess the gate** of their enemies."*

Genesis 22:17

The 18th President of the United States of America, Ulysses S. Grant, describe the ***"Art of War"*** as such: "locate your enemy, get at him as soon as you can, strike him as hard as you can and keep moving." This insight allows us to prepare strategies to engage our enemy in battle. The above scripture assures us that because we are the seed of Abraham, the promise that G-d made in **Gen. 22:17** applies to us today. We shall possess the gate of them that hate us, but we must first locate the enemy in our spiritual environment.

Sun Tzu's "The Art of War", informs us that an army is destroyed from implosion. Many marriages, ministries and business have dissolved because of the betrayal from within. Imploding comes in many forms, some of which are a breakdown in communication, lack of trust, greed, jealousy, etc.; causing strife, bitterness, hatred to form an alliance and destroy the army from the inside out!

This prophetic declaration spoken to Abraham has great implication, because it was reverberated to Rebecca just two versus later. It was an assurance concerning his posterity in the land.

T he angel of the Lord swore by nothing greater than the Lord, declaring that the seed of Abraham would possess the gate of the enemy. So what does possessing the gate of your enemy entail? It requires watchmen to move beyond status quo and occupy until the Lord returns (Lk. 19:13). Prophetic watchmen must possess the gates of the 7 mountains in our culture. The gates represent a place of adjudication/municipal law courts, (Is. 29:21; Amos 5:15; Zech. 8:16); a marketplace where commodities are bought and sold (II Kings 7:1; Nehemiah 12:25). The gates are the center for political activity and where the pulse of the people is examined (Judges 5:11; II Sam. 19:8). But they are also indicative of media and entertainment, because the Lord commanded the prophets the make public declarations at the city gates (Jer. 7:2 & 17:19).

The Army of the Lord is arising to take territory and move the boundary stones in the earth realm until there is an alignment with the decrees of Heaven. That is why we are the salt of the earth and the light of the world. Yes, prayer is necessary, & coupled with strategic intercession it is powerful and valuable. None would dispute that fact that intimacy is the cry of the Lord's heart for us and all of these are requirements as a prophetic watchman. But there is a dawning of a new day and the Lord is beckoning us to possess the gates of business, education, family, religion, sports, media/entertainment and the political arena. We are to be like the elders of old and influence decisions at the city gates. For some of us, the SET TIME is now! Take what we learned in our places of secrecy and "go then, and every place where the sole of your foot treads, and take territory for your King!"(Deut. 11:24 & Jos. 1:1-3)

POSSESSING THE GATES

Now the gates of Jericho were tightly shut because the people were afraid of the Israelites. No one was allowed to go out or in.
Joshua 6:1 (NLT)

G-d's judgment upon Jericho was 440 years in the making. According to Genesis 15, G-d told Abram that after four generations, his descendants would return to this land, after the sin had run its course. When Joshua sent spies into the city of Jericho in Joshua 2, Rahab declares how the Lord had parted the Red Sea for the Israelites, causing fear to grip the inhabitants of Jericho. The Lord had given all of Canaan an opportunity to repent, even up until six days before the walls fell. Their disobedience coupled with Joshua's obedience unto the word of G-d created a victory for the Israelites that is still unprecedented today.

The **FAITH** of the Israelites was unwavering as they submitted to the instructions of Joshua and allowed the Lord to fight their battle. You must understand that the walls of Jericho were said to be impregnable and thus the Israelites would not be able to penetrate the city gates. But I believe that when the commander of the Lord's army appeared to Joshua, he was accompanied by an array of heavenly host. The ground that Joshua stood on was Holy, because the Lord of Host was fighting this battle. The sin of Canaan was filled to its measure and the Lord's servant was about to execute judgment at HIS decree.

You may be wondering, how do we possess that gates in the 21st century, because our fight is not against "flesh and blood, but against the rulers, against the powers, against the world forces of this darkness, against the spiritual forces of wickedness in the heavenly places" *(Eph. 6:12).*

Possessing the gate is symbolic of the authority given to us by Jesus Christ. When we possess the gates of our enemy, we essentially operate in the authority entrusted to us. According to Luke 10:19, Jesus said, **"Behold, I give you the authority to trample on serpents and scorpions, and over all the power of the enemy, and nothing shall by any means hurt you."** Jesus Christ has entrusted us with the authority to use His name, and G-d has decreed that the authority attached to the name of Jesus is above ALL other names in creation.

"Therefore, God has highly exalted Him and given Him the name which is above every name, that at the name of Jesus every knee should bow, of those in heaven, and of those on earth, and of those under the earth, and that every tongue should confess that Jesus Christ is Lord, to the glory of G-d the Father." *(Phil 2:9-11)*

We are to exert the authority of the name of Jesus as He has commanded. In JESUS name, we are commanded to cast out demons, bind the power of the enemy, and loose those who are bound. To operate in the authority of Jesus' name we must be one with Him, bound and yoked so that we are of one mind, with one heart and on one accord in all things. Every action requires a response and that response must be in **obedience** to the *action* of G-d's word.

Let's examine how Jesus possessed the gates of the enemy. Jesus had authority in the synagogue and temple *(religious gates);* the Sanhedrin counsel *(a political gate);* the marketplace *(an economic gate);* & He ministered freely to Roman soldiers *(military gates).*

The King of the kings possessed the gates of the enemy in His living, but his finest hour & final triumph was to die for all human-kind. In death, Jesus possessed the FINAL gates of death and hell *Rev. 1:18!* And now these gates, which our Lord declared would not be a hindrance to His church, gave way to the One who is declared in Psalm 107:16: "For He hath broken the gates of brass, and cut the bars of iron in sunder". Jesus Christ willingly laid down His life, and as our chief shepherd He could then claim "I am the door/gate; if anyone enters through Me, he will be saved, and will go in and out and find pasture" *John 10:7-9.*

Jesus' path to possessing the gates of the enemy was death, and ours will be no less. He took possession of man's final enemy and triumphed over it in resurrection power. Then Jesus made a proclamation to His church, "I also say to you that you are Peter, and upon this rock I will build My church; and the gates of Hades will not overpower it. I will give you the keys of the Kingdom of Heaven; and whatever you bind on earth shall have been bound in heaven, and whatever you loose on earth shall have been loosed in heaven. *Matt. 16:18-19*

We as the body of Messiah have the "Keys to the Kingdom" and must operate in the authority that Christ has imputed to us. The key is a badge of authority *(Lk. 11:52)*, and is used to open doors. Peter used the keys Christ gave him to open the door to the Jews on the Day of Pentecost (Acts 2) & to the Gentiles after the Lord had sent him a vision and an appeal from Cornelius (Acts 10). Jesus' authority is manifested through our obedience to the Word of G-d. Our dying to worldly things must be done daily, along with a self examination of our heart. **What are you doing with the keys Christ has given to you?**

GATEKEEPERS

So they and their sons had charge of the gates of the house of the Lord, even the house of the tent, as guards. 24 The gatekeepers were on the four sides, to the east, west, north and south.
I Chronicles 9:23-24

Gatekeepers where watchmen on the walls, that were stationed at all "four gates" geographically (N, S, E, W). Their hearts were fully committed to the Lords' will. As 21st century gatekeepers, we must eagerly await the Lord's return, while vigilantly watching for any approaching danger. "At that time the kingdom of heaven will be like ten virgins who took their lamps and went out to meet the bridegroom" *(Matt. 25:1)*. Like the FIVE wise virgins, we must always be prepared and continually remind others to be alert for no man knoweth the hour of the bridegrooms return...We must usher in the King of Glory!

As gatekeepers we must ensure and protect the holiness of G-d's house. Standing on the truth of G-d's Word, our heart must be consumed with the Fear of the Lord, coupled with knowledge & understanding of the Word of G-d. We must embody the Word and become one with it.

As gatekeepers, PROTECT the house of the Lord from corruption and worldly ideas. Uphold the truth of G-d's Word and do not waver. Protect the people from following lies, false ideologies and doctrine. Cling tightly to the Word of G-d, and declare HIS Word in the gates. You must keep the people from stumbling off the narrow path. Keep the Lord's sheep safe until He comes back again, always staying ready and looking out for your master to return. He has commanded us to watch for His return.

Gatekeepers were assigned to warn the inhabitants of impending danger, because if the enemy took the gates, he won the battle. These gates speak to strength as well as vulnerability of a city/nation. The gates of Jericho were believed to be an impregnable stronghold. However, Joshua 6 informs us that ANY gate/stronghold can be penetrated. Jesus already has the keys to hell and its' gates shall NOT prevail against the church (Matt. 16:18); & you are the church!

Spiritually, there are gates/entry ways to your body and soul, which the adversary attacks. In the natural, once a gate is conquered, the ruling authority sets up a hierarchal structure to govern the newly conquered territory. The same happens spiritually, with your body and soul. If the enemy conquers a gate, a ruling spirit is appointed as gatekeeper of that area, monitoring all activity.

That controlling/ruling spirit then determines who or what is allowed access to your body or soul. **Matthew 12:43-45** informs us of what happens with conquered gates that have not been rebuilt:

> Now when the unclean spirit goes out of a man, it passes through waterless places seeking rest, and does not find *it.* "Then it says, 'I will return to my house from which I came'; and when it comes, it finds *it* unoccupied, swept, and put in order. "Then it goes and takes along with it seven other spirits more wicked than itself, and they go in and live there; and the last state of that man becomes worse than the first. That is the way it will also be with this evil generation.

As stated earlier, gates represents places of authority & power and **I John 5:19 declares**, "We know we are of G-d, and that the whole world lies in the power of the evil one." Our weapons of warfare are spiritual, not physical. II Cor. 10:3-5 states, "For though we walk in the flesh, we do not war according to the flesh, for the weapons of our warfare are not of the flesh, but divinely powerful for the destruction of fortresses. *We are* destroying speculations and every lofty thing raised up against the knowledge of God, and *we are* taking every thought captive to the obedience of Christ

To control the gate of a city is to CONTROL the city. The gates of the enemy shall be taken by G-d's people according to Nahum 2:6. G-d has already promised us that He will break the gates of the enemy for His people. Fortify your gates with the Word of G-d, remain one with Him and watch for approaching danger, for the enemy is seeking whom he may devour. ."

Chapter 5

RELEASING THE
WATCHMAN TO WAR

...Come quickly, all you nations everywhere! Gather together in the valley.
"And now, O LORD, call out your warriors!
Joel 3:11 (NLT)

T
he purpose of a prophetic intercessor who hedges up the breach, is that of spiritual warfare. In this arena, intercessors do not face G-d in prayer as they would in supplication; but instead, we turn and face the forces of evil and war the good fight of faith. The watchman's role is a warrior enforcing the authority entrusted to us by Christ's victory, which was won in HIS death and resurrection!

As prophetic intercessors, many of us are watchmen for our families, cities and nation, keeping vigil against an unseen enemy. Through the eyes of the spirit, we are able to sight impending danger and sound an alarm when needed. You are being released in this hour to fulfill the words that Ezekiel spoke:

> "Son of man, speak to the sons of your people and say to them, 'If I bring a sword upon a land, and the people of the land take one man from among them and make him their watchman, and he sees the sword coming upon the land and blows on the trumpet and warns the people, then he who hears the sound of the trumpet and does not take warning, and a sword comes and takes him away, his blood will be on his own head. He heard the sound of the trumpet but did not take warning; his blood will be on himself. But had he taken warning, he would have delivered his life. But if the watchman sees the sword coming and does not blow the trumpet and the people are not warned, and a sword comes and takes a person from them, he is taken away in his iniquity; but his blood I will require from the watchman's hand.' **(Ezekiel 33:2-6)**

Alarge s prophetic watchmen, you are appointed to various geographical locations and assignments to hedge up the **breach** in the wall; where structures have shifted and fallen into disarray. Your engagement in spiritual warfare is your ability to stand in the gap and close up the enemies breach into your church, city, or nation. You have been hidden in the caves for a season, but it is time for you to pronounce what the Lord is saying for this hour. If you do not sound the trumpet and warn G-d's people of impending danger, the accountability of what you see is charged to you.

Watchmen not only warn of impending danger, we also have the privilege of announcing the arrival of important Kingdom Ambassadors (Is. 52:7, 8). Two New Covenant watchmen saw the coming of the Messiah. On the day of His arrival in Jerusalem, both Anna and Simeon announced His entry to all who would listen (Lk. 2:25-38). G-d sets watchmen in their places upon the walls, and He requires that we take our job seriously (Is. 62:6-7).

Like Ezekiel, you are appointed as a watchman for where the Lord has designated; so when you hear a message from His mouth, you proclaim it in the gates that He has assigned to you. As watchmen, we are prayer warriors and intercessors functioning within our destiny, calling, assignment and inheritance. We know who we are in Christ and therefore die to self daily. Like Jesus, we are obedient to do what we see and hear the Father doing... for **Obedience** is greater than sacrifice. **BE PROPHETIC!**

Thy Kingdom Come, Thy Will Be Done, On Earth as it is in Heaven...

References

Eckhardt, John. *The Shamar Prophet.* (2006). The Crusaders Ministries.

Pierce, Chuck, Heidler Robert & Heidler, Linda. A Time To Advance
(2011). Glory of Zion International.
https://gloryofzion.org//webstore/Scripts/prodView.asp?idprod
uct=1112

Roberts, Wess. *Leadership Secrets of Attila the Hun.* (1985). Warner Books,
Inc.

Sun-Tzu. & Sawyer, Mei-chun. & Sawyer, Ralph D. & Sun Pin. (1996). T*he
complete art of war.* Boulder, Colo: Westview Press

Warfare. (n.d.). Dictionary.com Unabridged. Retrieved April 28, 2013,
from Dictionary.com
website: http://dictionary.reference.com/browse/warfare

http://www.brainyquote.com/quotes/authors/u/ulysses_s_grant.html

http://classic.studylight.org

http://www.merriam-webster.com/dictionary/reconnaissance

www.ingramcontent.com/pod-product-compliance
Lightning Source LLC
Chambersburg PA
CBHW061758040426
42447CB00011B/2360